Beginner's Guide
to Loss in the Multiverse

Poems by
Claudine Nash

BLUE LIGHT PRESS ◆ 1ST WORLD PUBLISHING

1st WORLD
PUBLISHING

SAN FRANCISCO ◆ FAIRFIELD ◆ DELHI

Winner of the 2020 Blue Light Book Award

Beginner's Guide to Loss in the Multiverse

BLUE LIGHT PRESS
www.bluelightpress.com
bluelightpress@aol.com

1ST WORLD PUBLISHING
PO Box 2211
Fairfield, IA 52556
www.1stworldpublishing.com

BOOK & COVER PHOTO & DESIGN
Melanie Gendron
melaniegendron999@gmail.com

AUTHOR PHOTO
Kate Chittenden

FIRST EDITION

Library of Congress Control Number: 2020942149

ISBN: 978-1-4218-3669-0

For all the M's

Table of Contents

IV. A Stunning Matter

"Outside the boundaries of the universe lie the raw realities, the could-have-beens, the might-bes, the never-weres, the wild ideas, all being created and uncreated chaotically like elements in fermenting supernovas. Just occasionally where the walls of the worlds have worn a bit thin, they can leak in."

Terry Pratchett

1.

Beginner's Guide to Loss in the Multiverse

Beginner's Guide to Loss in the Multiverse, Universe 415

*Beginner's Guide to Loss
in the Multiverse*, page 26:

I accept this challenge
of surrendering
all of you, every
notion of us
that could exist
in some other time
or space,

but recklessly
allow myself
two pieces of light;

the one that burst
from your eyes
the day we watched
the dust whirl

and saw all our
lives at once,

then later,
those particles that
slipped around you
as you stepped
into the distance.

I tell you,
never try to pocket

a photon.

Weeks afterwards,
these memories split
into ten thousand
streams that flooded
my sleep,

spilling bands
of hazel and loss
into the night.

Classic rookie
mistake.

Plastic Endings
Universe 11,098

A friend let it slip
that she later

walked in on you
playing with my

micro robots. This
scrap of unexpected

intelligence admittedly
made me cry. A

steel-eyed diminutive
pair one half-inch

in height, their
invasion of your

fingertips had
launched the tail

end of our false
parting.

Synapses charged
with disquiet, I

pitched their handoff
without any particular

elegance or aim,
blurting some absurdity

 like "take these
buggers with you"

because I couldn't
ask you to keep them

in a sad and
hallowed place.

You needn't had
been so scared.

Since You Left,
Universe 11,099

Today I walked in

    on the house robot

whispering your

    favorite sonnet.

This, after tracing

    your name in day-old

oil all along

    the attic walls.

I try to comfort her,

    though she would

sooner see me

    swallowed by

the moon. I

    lay my hand

upon the crack

in her back

that she suffered

the first time

you took her ice

skating, but she

spits obscene

strings of zeros

at me as though

I am a pile of

wasted silicon,

as though my heart

isn't already

twisted into a

mournful jumble

of spent circuits,

as if I alone could

have stopped you

from running.

Since You Left
Universe 11,100

The toothless
pterosaur
you used
to feed
keeps crying
for your
cold corn
and sardine
soup.
I spent
the morning
in the side
garden
grinding
insects,
dicing
scallions
and bits of
fresh fish,
yet still
he spits
my sorry
excuse of
a stew into
the dunes.
I fear time
is finding
him growing
thin and
ornery.
It's not

my intent
to make
another
suffer
hunger,
but I must
admit I
love the way
his wings
make wind
when he
takeo off
bothered
and empty-
bellied.
Tomorrow
I will tuck
your recipe
book back
under my
mattress and
bring him
a basket
of bread
soaked in
salt water
instead.
I thought
you both
knew
I'm not
much of
a cook.

Roll the Tape
Universe 16,096

Stop. Now focus in
on the sense that rolls
from your lips.

Right there, between
those bands of static
interference, there,

between sips of
white wine sangria
and a broken stream
of words.

Now rewind. Look,
there's your form
bathed in grey, pointing
at the clear and obvious
present.

Now take it frame
by frame until you
see that shadowy
trace that drifts from
our muscles.

See how it rises
and falls into the grainy
space between us?

The story we saw
but never spoke.

Fingertips
Universe 18,197

Today I am thinking
mostly of your hands
or rather the way I
like to watch them
when you are typing
or tying knots or are
otherwise occupied
and how a story seems
to rise from your fingertips
when you touch certain
colors or cottons or
the other types of soft
fabrics that I tend
to want to crawl
under.

Today this story is
a warm orange and
smells something like
marigolds. It twists
and turns for a rocky
bit but overall is
quite beautiful and
has the type of cozy
ending that you would
want to wrap around
yourself when trying
to get to sleep on
a cold planet or
maybe just a plain
old regular planet but
on a night like
this when the steps
can't stop creaking.

I Pass You an Empty Sky
Universe 3,027,217

I just
love when
I pass you
an empty
sky

and you
spin it

then
hand me
back

a fistful
of stars.

Pretend that You are Talking
Universe 3,082,018

Pretend
that you are
talking

just

to me.

I will
kneel here
while you
tell me all
about
the stars

stuck

in your
heart. You

can loosen
your tongue
and let
their cold

light spill
into the space
between us. I

will listen to
your quiet
wind rise, I

will stay
here when
this storm

fills your
mouth with
ice and
sky.

You can
bring your
lips near
and let the
dark

slip

into my
ear.

Pretend I
see nothing
untouchable.
Pretend

that I am
holding

all these
icy parts
of you,

that when
I look
you in the
eye I am

watching

wild grass
sway,

I am
touching

a stunning

bit of
night.

A Space for Your Moments
Universe 3,082,019

I would like to gift you a space,
a room without tile or board

or screen, but with corners
where moments dangle. Do

not needlessly paint its worn
walls in gold. Your name is laced

through these moments, may they
swell in your basket. May they

fill your room with ice or
storm or sand or whatever

matter lies in their pieces.
Here is an angle of light. I

will sit here while you lift each
one and inspect their sharp and

beautiful edges. I will sit here
and we will let them all breathe.

Worse Off
Universe 12,147,046

Somewhere I might be
an introverted albino
on a South Beach street,
desperate to camouflage into clouds
or sink in hollow
of whitewashed sand,

or build my house
on dissolving ground and
watch the first floor plunge
through a void
as the surface layer
gradually gives way.

I could be a claustrophobic canary
indentured to a mine or
pet shop cage, or

find myself a rabid coyote
parched
before a desert pool.

I know
there are worse things
in the world than wanting you
this way,

but right now I feel

like a beautifully-robed
monk with Tourette's

who ticks and blurts "shitfuck"
all the hours of his silent
retreat.

Unlike Here
Universe 12,146,091

See, I still believe
that somewhere
we are breathing
a strange but shared
pocket of air.

Maybe this air
hangs heavy with
vapor, maybe it
resembles thick dust
or a fume. I've never
been a stickler
for specificity.

When we lie down
in what looks like grass
you braid my
hair or tentacles,

I run my lips
along your forehead,
the arcs of each
of your six
eyebrows.

II.

Magnolias

Magnolias
Universe 1,071

Listen, I

    need to say

just once in

    this lifetime,

that when I

    look at you

I see a

    landscape,

alive and

    soaked in

magnolias,

    where I find

myself home

    in fields I

have never

    and always

known, to

     which each

and every

     turn, I

return.

Magnolias
Universe 1,072

I look at you
and at once

all the gaps
and restless
spaces in me
settle into this
landscape,

I drift home
wrapped
in a blanket
of magnolias.

Magnolias
Universe 1,073

I offer you
an empty
field soaked
in cold
and drained
of color —

                                you fill
                                the bare
                                and icy
                                spaces with
                                magnolias

Magnolias
Universe 1,074

You looked up

and deep beneath
the rocks and stones
and bones of you,

I saw a field
I know I've travelled,

a magnificent landscape
more alive than
any orchard.

I tried to slip under
a blanket of
magnolia blooms,

but you turned your head
towards the night.

III.

Entanglement

Time Capsule
Universe 31,197

Consider that right now
somewhere
beneath a sycamore,

a trace of you
is drifting from the cracks
of an abandoned
cigar box.

As you sleep soundly
clear across the eastern
seaboard,

a stranger
with a rusted spade

is reaching down
to brush the earth
that has been weighing
upon its wooden lid
these nights.

Now she lifts this
muddy capsule,

she peels back its seal
ever so gingerly,

and the universe
reclaims the air
that sits inside.

This is how
you come to awaken
whole and weightless,

how when you raise
your eyes towards
the morning sky

up floats
a peace sign pendant;

your first forty-five;

an ink well;

a perfectly preserved set
of words and beliefs;

the self you buried,

intact
and free.

Gut Instinct
Universe 101,175

Some call it a hunch or a sixth sense. Maybe it's part premonition, part intuition, or it's just that knee-jerk response that leaves you insisting "this is not the way" or "something here's amiss." Some days it whispers "stay, stay" and suddenly from nowhere you think "I feel at home here. I never want to leave." Perhaps an entangled particle settles onto the tip of your finger and you touch a trace of a moment you've seen somewhere else or you converse with a stranger in a tea shop and know at once you've swapped blends with a kindred spirit. Imagine if you perceived that same insistent murmur the day I weighed the space between your arms and my torso swore "this, this is where I fit."

Once Upon a Particle
Universe 101,176

Perhaps tonight when
the stars and dust
align just right,

a strange particle
will settle onto the tip
of your finger and

you will touch a trace
of a moment that
unfolds somewhere
else. Maybe this trace

will lead you to a home
you know but have
never seen

where you will smell
an unusual bread
baking or find me

gathering lilacs
or something resembling
dogwood blossoms

in the garden
behind the kitchen.

Perhaps I will lay
those branches down

and run my thumb
across that fingertip,

maybe you will
carry this moment
long after the wind
returns it to the universe.

Perhaps you will lay
your own thumb
over this moment
and feel more
than skin;

you will detect
a floral scent rising
between ice crystals
and touch a trace
of me.

Entanglement
Universe 191,177

On this ground I plant
a seed.

I lay by this mound
of peat moss and earth
and await a garden,

I sense a wind.

In another realm
you step on a bed
of cracked clay
and smell peonies.

You breathe

and a trace
of hyacinth bursts
from the night.

Entanglement
Universe 191,178

You reach through
this spiral of settling light

and touch
a drifting,
mislaid piece
of dust.

You lift it

and somewhere else
in time and space,

something in me
rises.

IV.

A Stunning Matter

The Making of Memory
Universe 101,177

You are standing
in a moment

on my favorite
piece of
ground

under
an angle of
morning sun

I know
will come
to shift.

I hold
the light
here.

Strange but True
Universe 416

1. Once I lifted
a piece of the light
that streamed
between us and
stuck it in a
moment only I
could open.

2. This angle of light
is invading my
synapses. It does
not shift.

3. A rogue stream
of particles once
slipped through this
moment. Once
you looked at me
and that same piece
of light poured
from your
pupils.

A year later,
I dream of
nothing but
dust.

4. Those photons
became encased
in crystal. I leave
fingerprints all
over its surface,
everything I touch
feels like glass.

5. Last week it crept
into the garden
and wound its way
around the ivy.
Today, it spilled all
over the mint.
Now I can't
make mojitos.

6. Sometimes I hold
this moment
like a wandering
child. Granted,
my grip might be
a bit too tenacious.

7. I am releasing
it now, but dread
the dim gap
that lies beneath.
Oddly, I've
been known
to struggle a bit
with empty spaces.

8. Sometimes
I get a little
stuck.

Strange but True
Universe 7,893,459

Think of this moment
as ninety-eight percent
glass:

the light that spills
from your eyes as a
prism;

an infinite that unfolds
with the precision
of cut crystal;

the sudden transparency
in this glance.

Now step away
and hear the cracking
of chest muscles,

the separation of fibers,

a fracturing

as my heart sinks
through my bones
as a stone dropping.

Somewhere We Are Carpenters
Universe 69,693

Somewhere
we are
carpenters.

We pass
the morning
counting
footsteps,

calculating
cuts of pine
and oak,

beams
of knotted
barn wood

salvaged
from another
life.

Our tallies
drift upwards
as an echoing
mantra.

You lift
your eyes

and a home

bursts
from your
lips,

I whisper
a city

though
a room
of glassless
windows.

Somewhere We Are Carpenters
Universe 69,694

Somewhere else in time
I count stones

for the sake of hearing
something other than
my thoughts,

I climb these ruins
alone amongst a group
of others.

As I regard
the cloud bank
that rolls behind,

I imagine myself
a carpenter
rebuilding room
by room

the remains
of these ancient
homes.

For a moment,
I live in one
with you,

the traveler who takes
unsure steps

a hundred yards
ahead.

I am certain
I hear the numbers
in my mind
whispered from
above;

they echo
in the mist
then clip
towards me
down the footpath.

The Theory of Everything
Universe 4,752

Still I summon
that single moment
when you stood before me
and spoke a dialect
of silence
that had no such word
as never,
when you stared me
straight on
as the morning burst
around us,
and I swore
I heard the sound
of light.

The Theory of Everything
Universe 4,753

Once, you looked

            at me

                    and with

                            your eyes

                touched

            the need

         I cannot

    bear

to see,

      reached in

            without warning,

                        and lifted

           its stirring form

    from a long

and deadened

        sleep.

            This is why

                  now when

                        we meet,

                I stare at

           your knees,

        I make

      such lousy

eye contact.

It's a Given,
Universe 6

I love how
you indulge
all my loose
intrusive
moments.
Like when
I wake you
as the
storm shakes
the night
to ask
"for what
do you
still hunger?"
With weighted
eyelids
and breath
still full
of sleep,
you roll
closer and
whisper
"whirled
peas."

It's a Given,
Universe 7

Today

    oddly

        and

           without

              reason,

                  I awoke

              when

          the

        wind

     began

  to

     whirl

        through

           the

                thick

bands

of

sleet

and

inexplicably

found

myself

wanting

nothing

but

peas.

How I Lost All Interest in Telekinesis
Universe 2,013,051

If I mastered the art of
moving objects with my

      mind, I wouldn't

waste time
bending spoons or influencing

      the outcome of rolling

dice. I wouldn't
expend energy

      shifting knitting needles

or inciting molecules of air
to make wind. I'd outright

      refuse to raise

room temperature by
vibrating atoms (although

      I concede summoning lost

keys could come in handy
every now and again).

      If I were a paranormal whiz,

I'd rewrite you into the
laws of physics. I'd

      lift you up the northbound

thruway mid-phoneme,
half-formed thought,

      unbitten pastry in hand;

invoke you until you landed
feet first inches from my

      hauling eyes, your morning

tea still steeping.
Truth be told,

      I'm starting to think this

telekinetic, parapsychological
phenomenon is a

      pseudoscientific myth,

because if I had any real
remote mental influence,

      with all my wishing and wanting

and directed conscious intent,
you should have popped in

      aeons ago.

How Not to Flirt in the Multiverse
Universe 771,199

Baby, there's
a galaxy
spinning

in here
and when you
looked over

at me a
trillion lifetimes
just spilled

between us.
You are a
glorious

atmosphere,
an infinite
matter. Yes

Baby, that
one look
lifted all

my mislaid
pieces,
you breathe

and all the
dust in this
strange and

random
universe
rises.

Though
seriously,
all I really

want from
you is "yes"
or "now" or

alternatively
just a plain
old "infinite"

will more
than likely
do.

A Stunning Matter
Universe 6,196,396

See this patch of
of space and time?

You are the thread
that vibrates though
this fabric,

you are the knot
that that ties these
strands of light.

I am waiting
in the moment
that sits right here
between us.

Now lean in
and weave it into
a stunning matter.

Acknowledgements

Much appreciation to the editors of the following publications where many of these poems previously appeared mostly under different titles:

Ariel Chart, Avalon Literary Review, BlazeVOX, Breadcrumbs Magazine, Dime Show Review, Ethos Literary Journal, Foliate Oak Literary Magazine, Green Briar Review, S*tar*Line, Westchester Review* and *Yellow Chair Review*

"A Space for Your Moments" and "The Making of Memory" appeared in the chapbook *Things for Which You Thirst (*Weasel Press, 2020)

"Worse Off" and "How I Lost All Interest in Telekinesis" appeared in the chapbook *The Problem with Loving Ghosts* (Finishing Line Press, 2014).

An excerpt from the "Magnolias" series appeared in *The Wild Essential* (Aldrich Press, 2017).

An earlier version of "Gut Instinct Universe, 101,175" appeared in *Parts per Trillion* (Aldrich Press, 2016).

Special thanks to Bob Raymonda for creating *Breadcrumbs Magazine,* a publication of collaborative inspiration that drove me to write so many of these poems.

Much gratitude to the regulars For the Love of Words open mic nights (Ken Valenti, Susan Moorhead, Caroline Reddy, David Deutsch, Julianna Dawson, Mercy Tullis-Bukhari, Britt DiGiacomo, Angela Taylor, Kamilah Glover and others) for their friendship and support as well as to Scott Plous for his incredible belief in me and Carlos Monteagudo and his appreciation for all things multiverse.

And of course, much love to my family Chris and Ella Hackney, Stanley Nash, all the Petriccas and all the Katz, and to my beloved Karen Nash who I hope is reading this in some corner of the multiverse.

About the Author

Claudine Nash is a psychologist and award-winning poet whose collections include the full-length books *The Wild Essential* (Kelsay Books: Aldrich Press, 2017) and *Parts per Trillion* (Kelsay Books: Aldrich Press, 2016) as well as the chapbooks *Things for Which You Thirst* (Weasel Press, 2020) and The *Problem with Loving Ghosts* (Finishing Line Press, 2014). She also edited three poetry anthologies: *Epiphanies and Late Realizations of Love* (Transcendent Zero Press, 2019), *Destigmatized* (Madness Muse Press, 2017) and *In So Many Words* (Madness Muse Press, 2016). Her work has been nominated for the Pulitzer, Pushcart and Best of the Net Anthology Prizes and has earned numerous literary distinctions including prizes from such publications and artistic organizations as Artists Embassy International, Thirty West Publishing House, The Song Is…, and Eye on Life Magazine among others. Internationally published, her poetry has appeared in a wide range of magazines and anthologies.

CPSIA information can be obtained
at www.ICGtesting.com
Printed in the USA
FSHW011957260720
72489FS